# BUSINESS
# GERMANY

# BUSINESS GERMANY

## A Practical Guide to Understanding German Business Culture

Peggy Kenna     Sondra Lacy

*Printed on recyclable paper*

**PASSPORT BOOKS**
a division of *NTC Publishing Group*
Lincolnwood, Illinois USA

**Library of Congress Cataloging-in-Publication Data**

Kenna, Peggy.
    Business Germany: a practical guide to understanding German business
culture / Peggy Kenna, Sondra Lacy.
        p.    cm.
    ISBN 0-8442-3555-5
    1. Business etiquette—Germany.    2. Corporate culture—Germany.
    3. Business communication—Germany.    4. Negotiation in business—
    Germany.    I. Lacy, Sondra.    II. Title.
HF5389.K454    1994
395' .52'0943—dc20                                    93—40566
                                                                    CIP

Published by Passport Books, a division of NTC Publishing Group.
4255 West Touhy Avenue, Lincolnwood, (Chicago) Illinois 60646-1975, U.S.A.
©1994 by NTC Publishing Group. All rights reserved.
No part of this work may be reproduced, stored in a retrieval system
or transmitted in any form or by any means,
electronic or mechanical, including photocopying and recording or otherwise
without the prior permission of NTC Publishing Group.
Manufactured in the United States of America.

4 5 6 7 8 9 0 VP 9 8 7 6 5 4 3 2 1

# Contents

Peggy Kenna is a communication specialist working with foreign-born professionals in the American workplace. She provides cross-cultural training and consultation services to companies who are conducting business internationally. She is also a certified speech and language pathologist who specializes in accent modification. Peggy lives in Tempe, Arizona.

Sondra Lacy is a certified communications specialist and teaches American communication skills to foreign-born professionals in the American workplace. She also provides cross-cultural training and consultation services to companies conducting business internationally. Sondra lives in Scottsdale, Arizona.

*Business Germany* is an invaluable tool for thousands of entrepreneurs, businesspeople, corporate executives, technicians, and salespeople seeking to develop lasting business relationships in Germany.

The book provides a fast, easy way for you to become acquainted with business practices and protocol to help you increase your chances for success in Germany. You will discover the secrets of doing business internationally while improving your interpersonal communication skills.

Let this book work for you.

> Pam Del Duca
> President/CEO
> The DELSTAR Group
> Scottsdale, Arizona

Entrepreneur Of The Year®
Award Recipient

## Welcome to Business Germany

*Business Germany* offers a smooth and problem-free transition between the American and German business cultures.

This pocket-size book contains information you need when traveling in Germany or doing business with German colleagues. It explains the differences in business culture you will encounter in areas such as:

- Business etiquette

- Communication style

- Problem solving and decision making

- Meetings and presentation style

*Business Germany* gets you started on the right track and challenges you to seek ways to improve your success in the global marketplace by understanding cultural differences in the ways people communicate and do business with each other.

Successful international companies are able to adapt to the business styles acceptable in other countries and by other nationalities, based on their knowledge and awareness of key cultural differences. These differences, if not acknowledged and addressed, can interfere in successful communication and can adversely affect the success of any business attempting to expand internationally.

*Business Germany* is designed to overcome such difficulties by comparing the American culture with the culture of Germany. Identifying appropriate behavior in one's own culture can make it easier to adapt to that of the country with which you are doing business. With this in mind, the book's unique parallel layout allows an at-a-glance comparison of German business practices with those of the United States.

Practical and easy to use, *Business Germany* will help you win the confidence of German associates and achieve common business goals.

The global business environment today is a multicultural one. While general business considerations are essentially the same the world over, business styles differ greatly from country to country. What is customary and appropriate in one country may be considered unusual or even offensive in another. The increasingly competitive environment calls for an individual approach to each national market. The success of your venture outside your home market depends largely upon preparation. The American style of business is not universally accepted. Yet we send our employees, executives, salespeople, technicians to negotiate or carry out contracts with little or no understanding of the cultural differences in the ways people communicate and do business with each other. How many business deals have been lost because of this cultural myopia?

Globalization is a process which is drawing people together from all nations of the world into a single community linked by the vast network of communication technologies. Technological breakthroughs in the past two decades have made instant communication between individuals around the world an affordable reality.

As these technological advances continue to open up and expand the dialogue among members of the world community, the need for effective communication between nations and peoples has accelerated.

When change occurs as dramatically and rapidly as we have witnessed in the past decade, many people throughout the world are being forced to quickly learn and adapt to unfamiliar ways of doing things. Some actually welcome change and the opportunities it presents, while others are reluctant to give up familiar ways of doing things. History proves that cultures are slow to change. But, individuals who are mentally prepared to accept change and deal with differences can successfully adapt to cultures very different from their own.

A culture develops when individuals have common experiences and share their reactions to these experiences by communicating with other members of their society.

Over time, communication becomes the vehicle by which cultural beliefs and values are developed, shared and transmitted from one generation to the next.

Effective communication between governments or international businesses requires more than being able to speak the language fluently or relying on expert interpreters. Understanding the language is only the first step. Understanding and accepting the behaviors, customs and attitudes of other cultures while doing business globally is also required to bring harmony and success in the worldwide business and political arena.

The importance of the influence of one's native culture on the way one approaches life cannot be overstated. Each country's cultural beliefs and values are reflected in people's idea of the "right" way to live and behave.

In general, businesspeople who practice low-key, non-adversarial, win/win techniques in doing business abroad tend to be most successful. Knowing what your company wants to achieve, its bottom line, and also understanding the objectives of the other party and helping to accommodate them in the business transaction is necessary for developing long-term, international business relationships.

Often, representatives from American companies, for example, have difficulty doing business with *each other*, even when they speak the same language and share a common culture. Consider how much more difficult it is to do business with people from different cultures who speak different languages.

Success in the international business arena will not be easy for those who do not take steps to gain the skills necessary to be global players. The language barrier is an obvious problem.

Equally important will be negotiation skills, as well as an understanding of and adaptation to the social and business etiquette of the foreign country. Americans have a reputation for failing to appreciate this. In other words, businesspeople doing business abroad will get off to a good start if they remember to do the following:

- Listen closely; understand the verbal and non-verbal communications.
- Focus on mutual interests, not differences.
- Nurture long-term relationships.
- Emphasize quality. Be prepared to defend the quality of your products and services, and the quality of your business relationship.

ISO 9000 is fast becoming a universal passport for doing business in Europe. ISO stands for International Organization for Standardization.

This is a new set of concise standards covering documented quality control systems for product development, design, production, management and inspection.

## Doing Business in a Global Market

The European Economic Community (EEC) has adopted ISO certification and more than 20,000 European companies are complying. Increasing numbers of European companies are refusing to do business with foreign suppliers who don't meet ISO standards. Product areas under the most pressure to comply include automotive, aerospace, electronics, testing and measuring instruments, and products where safety and reliability can become an issue. Companies with Total Quality Management (TQM) in place find it easier to pass ISO 9000 audits.

Successful companies will need to adapt to these rules and standards set by Europe in order to do business there.

Total Quality Management is becoming an integral part of successful companies in the U.S.

TQM is an organized, company-wide effort to eliminate waste in every aspect of business and produce the highest quality product possible. TQM is a philosophy that focuses on the customer, manages by facts, empowers people and improves processes.

Implementation of TQM is a real challenge and requires a company commitment to invest the time and finances necessary to reshape the entire organization. How is this accomplished? Through a team approach which values customer and employee opinions and in which everyone is committed to identify waste and its root cause and correct it in a timely manner. An effective tool for accomplishing this is through brainstorming efforts allowing everyone to participate. The successful TQM company is customer driven and uses leadership, information and analysis, strategic quality planning, human resource utilization, and quality assurance of products and services to reach goals.

Total Quality Management is a survival tool for businesses in a global market.

Germany has been the richest, strongest, most efficient, orderly, productive, scientifically and technically advanced, and most populous country in Europe. Unification has had a profound impact on the country and the ramifications of this change must be watched if you are going to do business there. It is no longer business as usual but some business practices have remained the same, such as working with government agencies.

Even with the problems of unification, Germany is considered the leading economic power in Europe today and a dominant force worldwide. Its currency has been among the strongest and most stable of any European nation, and it is one of the world's foremost exporter of manufactured goods.

Germany is considered a model of Western capitalism, a position supported by a large and prosperous middle class. Labor/management relations have been generally harmonious because German law has given workers much participation and protection. Education plays a major role in Germany and its literacy rate is very high.

Banks dominate business. Their role is as the principal provider of funds. Germans are very conservative and do not have many entrepreneurial or innovative enterprises

The government of Germany has made a major investment in business which has led to many regulations which are adhered to. Germany's expertise is in the "smokestack" industries. Their great strength is that they do things the "old fashioned" way and do them very well. Quality and craftsmanship are very important to them.

There is a very close relationship between the government and the business community which is not present in America.

Germany is a hard country to define; it continues to change. It is also a country which in many ways is very similar to the U.S., but do not assume that they do business the American way or that they feel the same way Americans do about business.

*Remember that within a culture, there are individual differences among people and within business organizations. Be prepared to find specific exceptions to the general trends within a culture.*

### United States

#### ■ *Friendly and informal*

Americans are a very friendly and informal people but these traits can sometimes seem overly familiar and intrusive to others. Americans also tend to be very open in their relationships. They usually share family and work experience easily. The design of most American offices encourages peer/colleague interaction. But Americans do tend to avoid close personal relationships in business.

The United States is a very mobile society and Americans are used to meeting and dealing with strangers.

Touching is tolerated socially but could be construed as sexual harassment in the workplace. Americans use direct eye contact.

Americans believe that competition encourages improvement and innovation. They do not hesitate to confront others.

Duty and obedience are valued but loyalty must be earned.

# Germany

## ■ *Reserved and formal*

Germans tend to take themselves very seriously. They emphasize good manners and do not like American informality or calling each other by first names.

Space is sacred, including office space. German employees tend to keep doors closed to provide boundaries and minimize interruptions. Their personal space tends to be slightly greater than Americans.

German society has not been very mobile in the past and many are not used to dealing with strangers. Those who have extensive dealings with foreigners have learned to be more open and friendly, and if they have studied English will often want to practice their language skills.

Germans tend to dislike touching but do use direct eye contact. They have a strong sense of privacy. They do not like questions about family, personal life, etc. It is best to stick to business topics. They tend to avoid personal relationships in business.

Germans believe in cooperation, not competition. They are very conformist. They dislike personal confrontation but do not hesitate to point out if a foreigner does not meet acceptable behavior. Duty, obedience and loyalty are highly valued.

# Communication Style

## United States

### ■ *Look inward*

Americans have traditionally been more interested in what happens within their country's borders than in the rest of the world. They have been historically and politically naive about European affairs, but recently many are recognizing the necessity of becoming better informed about other countries of the world.

### ■ *Direct*

Americans like to state their purpose right away and want to get right down to business (get to the point). Timelines are very important.

Americans use small talk for developing rapport in order to work together more effectively. They are more comfortable meeting strangers and use small talk to get to know someone.

## ■ *Historical outlook*

When Germans explain something they often find it necessary to lay a proper foundation and historical context. They will often give a lengthy background explanation with many references to past history. They, like many of the European nations, are well informed as to what is happening in the rest of Europe and the rest of the world.

## ■ *Blunt*

Many Germans tend to be more frank than Americans may be used to. They can sometimes be seen by others as insensitive and pushy.

Traditionally Germans have not used much "small talk." They often are not comfortable with strangers and may find it difficult to talk to them. As Germans deal more with foreigners this is changing.

They like people who are very clear about their expectations and, like Americans, they want to get right down to business.

# Communication Style

## United States

### ■ *Prone to overstatement*

Although Americans want to downplay the emotional aspects of business, they tend to be outgoing and, especially in sales, like to embellish or boast about their accomplishments, their company and its products and services. Today many businesses are starting to be conducted more on the reliability and integrity of a company and its products.

### ■ *Clear and concise*

Americans tend to feel that both written and oral presentations should be brief and easy to understand. It is not as important to look organized as to be organized. Some people can look very disorganized and still be effective.

## ■ *Tend to be understated*

Germans like people who are clear about their expectations and who downplay feelings or the emotional aspect of business. They are apt to soft pedal their statements and dislike boasting. The reliability and integrity of a company are very important.

## ■ *Well organized and systematic*

Germans not only like people who are organized but who look organized. Germans have a tendency to feel that the more difficult a piece of writing is to understand, the more valuable the ideas. They regard concise writing as simple minded. They also dislike overstatement. They tend to not readily accept new information but are very persevering and persistent when assessing new situations and information.

## United States

### ■ *Communication important*

Depending on the individual company, information can be used as power and not shared freely, or it may be shared more freely. Power flows from the top down or into matrix management depending on the preference of the chief executive or owner of the company.

American managers hold employees responsible for their performance but employees also tend to like some supervision.

Americans can become territorial when under much stress and uncertainty.

### ■ *Quick decision making*

Americans tend to like making quick decisions. Since a certain amount of failure is permissible, these decisions can be easily changed if it appears things are not working. Americans also feel that problems or mistakes can be fixed as they arise.

Americans want to accomplish the job with a minimum expenditure of time and effort.

## ■ *Information is power*

Hierarchy is important in German businesses. Power is often more visible than in the U.S. and flows from top down and moves slowly through many layers of management. Information is not always shared freely but provided on a need-to- know basis. This can sometimes result is a lack of information among workers.

German companies hold their employees responsible for their individual performance but do not provide a lot of supervision. They expect departments to solve their own problems. Germans can be highly territorial.

## ■ *Decision making slow but firm*

Decision making in many German companies is cautious, containing many fallback positions, contingency plans and alternatives. Germans tend to dislike trial and error techniques or using intuitive thinking to solve problems.

Decision making is also slow since Germans need to build consensus with those who will implement the decision. Once a decision is made, Germans stand firmly and unalterably behind it.

### United States

#### ■ *Decision making at all levels*

Individual decision making is seen as efficient and one person is usually given power to make the final decision and bear all responsibility. There is always a clear decision maker. Decision makers are found at all levels depending on the importance of the decision. Lower levels often get a chance to provide input; Americans believe that those closest to a problem should have input into the solution. Brainstorming is often part of the decision-making process.

#### ■ *Boss expected to be management expert*

In the upper ranks of management, promotion is often not based on technical expertise or competence but instead is based on things like good management skills, ability to "play the game," and such. Managers delegate responsibilities in the technical area. Delegating can be written or spoken.

Criticism is given readily but not always received easily.

## ■ *Decisions are from top down*

The decision-making process requires many clearances, background research and is approached slowly. It is orderly, organized and logical.

Decisions are made at the top in German companies but implementation is delegated and is fairly quick. There are clear decision makers here, too.

## ■ *Boss expected to be technical expert*

Germans value highly technical and factual expertise. Heads of companies tend to be engineers or economists who are very loyal to their products and their employees. They are very unlikely to consult management personnel for advice on running the company.

Delegation is clear, precise and preferably written. Subordinates will rarely question the boss.

Criticism is seldom given or received easily.

## United States

### ■ *Directive management*

American industry has been hierarchical although it is becoming less so. In American companies someone is always in charge. Whoever is put in charge of implementing a decision is expected to be completely accountable for its success or failure. Decisions do tend to go from the top down, but decision makers are found at all levels depending on the importance of the decision. Organizational structure is often changed.

Recently Total Quality Management (TQM) is being used by many of the larger companies.

### ■ *Planning*

Planning in American companies tends to be short term and is usually market driven.

Planning is usually determined by top management but the team which has to implement the plan is often consulted. Complete consensus, however, is not required.

## ■ *Hierarchical management*

German companies usually have a board of directors which runs the company. Below this ruling board the company is organized in a strict vertical hierarchy. Job positions are compartmentalized which tends to restrict information flow.

Many decisions which might be considered routine by Americans must be referred to top management. This can slow down negotiations. Top management feels lower levels shouldn't be bothered with bigger issues.

## ■ *Planning*

Planning is done by senior management but requires complete consensus from those who will carry it out. Germans are very good at long-term planning but sometimes lack the flexibility and quick reactions necessary to deal with sudden problems that come up. German companies tend to be engineering driven.

## United States

### ■ *Constant change*

Americans tend to see change as good, although constant change causes established hierarchies and relationships to be repeatedly disrupted. The needs of the individual are subsidiary to the organization. Loyalty between employee and company is temporary but expected to be wholehearted while it lasts.

America was developed by risk takers and this trait is still highly valued.

## ■ *Like stability*

Germans tend to dislike uncertainty and ambiguity and unquantifiable risk. They like security and dislike making mistakes. They are not partial to improvising and are generally not risk takers but prefer traditional approaches. They have not been particularly flexible but are getting better at adapting since their country has been changing rapidly. It has become essential for Germans to become more adaptable and flexible as they work on solving their reunification problems.

German management tends to be very loyal to highly valued and esteemed customers.

# Organizational Structure

## United States

### ■ *Pragmatic*

Americans value what works rather than theory. They also believe that it is OK to take chances and learn from mistakes. Americans also value resourcefulness, innovation and resilience.

### ■ *Teamwork valued*

Teams are used to define or reach specific goals and each individual on the team has a specific job to make the goal attainable. Within teams, people still function as individuals. Americans tend to balance the needs of the team with individual needs. Promotions are earned through competence and political savvy.

### ■ *Impatient*

Americans have tended to be more impulsive and spontaneous; they want to "do" something and do not want to calmly wait for something to happen.

Americans will often take the initiative when dealing with change or with the unexpected.

## ■ *Perfectionist*

Germans conduct business with great attention to order and planning. They demand high quality, long lasting goods, and abhor waste. They have a strong need to be correct and dislike making mistakes or having them pointed out. They rarely compliment although some are getting better at this.

## ■ *Individual orientation*

People strive for individual achievement and are not particularly oriented to teamwork. Promotion is earned through competence and pay is related to individual performance.

## ■ *Careful*

Germans tend to be cautious, orderly and pay great attention to detail. Taking the initiative is not encouraged; Germans are highly disciplined and believe in sticking closely to the rules. They do not like dealing with the unexpected. German companies are well suited to manufacturing where major decisions have a long life span.

### United States

#### ■ *Appointments*

Appointments are generally kept and punctuality is fairly important.  Being a few minutes late (depending on the circumstances) is usually not frowned on.

#### ■ *Quick planning/implementation*

Planning and implementation is usually fairly quick in American companies. Americans attempt to stick to schedules.   But a certain amount of failure to meet a schedule is allowed.

## ■ *Appointments*

Germans are very meticulous about appointments. They are made far in advance and everything must be planned out.

Punctuality is very important. Do not be late. Meetings will start and end on time even if its aims are not accomplished.

## ■ *Precise scheduling*

Germans tend to take longer to plan and to implement those plans but they are very time conscious and will stick rigidly to the agreed-upon schedule.

### United States

#### ■ *Fast pace*

Americans tend to make quick decisions. They are also pragmatic; if something isn't working, they will quickly change the approach. This allows Americans to respond more quickly to a changing market. They also look for immediate results.

#### ■ *Energetic*

Americans are a nation of doers. They like to see action and progress, sometimes at the expense of quality. They sometimes will support action that seems to be effective, even though it may not appear to be the efficient way to do things.

## ■ *Deliberate*

Expect decision making to take longer in Germany. German businesses plan for the future, methodically building a solid foundation. They have not been preoccupied with immediate results like Americans, but are becoming more aware of adjusting their philosophy to the changing market.

## ■ *Efficient*

Quality is very important to Germans. They also like to be able to accomplish the job as efficiently and effectively as possible.

## United States

### ■ *Used as communication tool*

Some meetings are brainstorming meetings; some are to persuade; some are to disseminate information; some are to discuss, defend and decide. Meetings can become very heated with confrontations and disagreements to be resolved. Ad hoc committee meetings are common. Meetings can be formal or informal, depending upon leadership style.

## ■ *Used to give information*

The people who attend a meeting are seen as a group of individuals each with a given expertise under a strong leader and with a specific objective. Everything must have a place in the timetable and organizational chart. Ad hoc committee meetings are not common.

The decision-making process is usually carried out by the relevant experts before the meeting. At the meeting the senior person is expected to clearly and concisely explain what decisions were reached. He does not need to elaborate or persuade. If a meeting consists of peers only, then some debate is allowed. Everyone is expected to come well prepared to speak. Germans will only agree to what they feel they can carry out.

### United States

#### ■ *Joking common*

Americans believe joking relieves stress and keeps relations informal and friendly and therefore are known for joking during informal meetings. In formal meetings or presentations, joking will be minimal or absent. It may take place after the formal meeting/presentation in concluded.

#### ■ *Flexible*

Each company in the U.S. has a little different protocol. Americans like agendas but are willing to change them. Everyone is expected to take notes and ask questions. Americans tend to adapt to fit the demanded or perceived protocol.

## ■ *Very serious*

Germans do not tend to joke during a meeting or presentation, but this is changing somewhat.

## ■ *Formal*

Germans like to get right down to business with minimum pleasantries. Although Germans usually have an agenda and take minutes, this may not always be true. Attendees should ask permission before taking notes at a meeting.

### United States

#### ■ *Presentations*

Americans tend to have a projecting style of presentation. They often combine informative and persuasive styles as an efficient method of presentation. They attempt to persuade the audience to make a decision or take an action at the same time as they provide information. They consider this an effective and efficient use of time. Americans also believe in the "hard sell" and "quick close" approach to selling. They expect the audience to ask questions and to test the presenter's knowledge. Presenters expect to defend their opinions.

Americans also tend to be factual and inductive. They like to present their data clearly. They like summaries and often give the conclusion first and then tell how that conclusion was reached. They like to use visuals to inform and clarify.

## ■ *Presentations*

Germans believe presentations should be well thought out, carefully researched, thorough and orderly. They like facts and more facts and examples. They appreciate presentations which give them lots of information and summarize all main points at the end. They also tend to take longer to get to the point and it usually comes at the end of a presentation. Impromptu presentations are not appreciated.

Germans have a forceful manner of speaking but tend to use restrained gestures. Statements delivered with a positive air are more likely to be believed. They dislike the hard sell but like efficiency, performance, and quality emphasized. They like the use of visuals. It is very important to give the impression of being thoroughly prepared; this is also true with written materials.

Although asking questions during a presentation is often acceptable, Germans do not like a confrontational attitude by the questioner.

## United States

### ■ *Competitive*

Americans are very competitive and want to get the best deal. Like Germans, they are not particularly relationship oriented. However, Americans can be fairly flexible in order to conclude a business transaction. They also tend to be more spontaneous in their approach to negotiations rather than engaging in a lot of planning. They are often fairly informal in their approach to negotiations.

Americans tend to be more market driven and like information on marketing products as much as getting technical details.

### ■ *Risk takers*

Americans have generally been very interested in anything new and have been more apt to take risks.

## ■ *Hard bargainers*

Germans are very well prepared and serious about negotiations. They will be thoroughly knowledgeable about products and contract details. They look for proposals to be detailed, logical and filled with technical information; they also want them to be concrete and realistic. If you're selling to the Germans, you should research their markets thoroughly.

Germans are very good at squeezing concessions no matter how much they like your products or services. They are particularly fond of asking for last-minute concessions. So it is best to always hold a little something in reserve. It is also imperative to know your bottom line when negotiating with the Germans.

It's a good idea to take along technical people as part of the negotiating team since the Germans like a lot of technical information.

## ■ *Financially conservative*

Germans are not risk takers. They like to invest in sound projects with sound financing and a good chance for profit. They are primarily interested in foreign companies who can supply something they don't have, especially leading-edge technology.

## United States

### ■ *Profit oriented*

American companies are usually very concerned with money and the bottom line. Their primary concern is with profit. Money is seen as a sign of success which gives status. Americans are concerned with getting the best deal they can and with winning.

### ■ *Decision making*

Decisions during negotiations do not always need to be made by executives but can often be made by lower level managers; consensus is not necessary either.

Decision making can also be much quicker since Americans are often quite impatient to get the deal concluded.

## ■ *Quality and schedules important*

To do business with the Germans you must convince them that your company can maintain consistent quality standards. The Germans also put pressure on delivery dates and may ask for penalty clauses to ensure that agreed upon dates are met. They may also ask for a generous warranty to assure that quality standards are met. Their contracts will be very detailed as a result of this.

## ■ *Decision making*

Decision making in German companies involves a thorough analysis of all facts which have been presented during negotiation sessions. They like to have the other side leave as much written material as possible for them to study, and it is also a good idea to summarize all meetings in writing.

As a result, decision making takes time. They also may need to clear decisions at the top.

# U.S. Business Etiquette

- Be punctual. Americans are very time conscious. They also tend to conduct business at a fairly fast pace.

- A firm handshake and direct eye contact is the standard greeting.

- Direct eye contact is very important in business. Not making eye contact implies boredom or disinterest.

- Gift giving is not common. The United States has bribery laws which restrict the value of gifts which can be given.

- The United States is not particularly rank and status conscious. Titles are not used when addressing executives. Americans usually like to use first names very quickly. Informality tends to be equated with equality.

- Business meetings usually start with a formal agenda and tasks to be accomplished. There is usually very little small talk. Participants are expected to express their ideas openly; disagreements are common.

- If there is no one to introduce you at a business meeting, it is acceptable to introduce yourself and present your card.

- Permission should be asked before smoking.

## German Business Etiquette

- A firm handshake is the rule.
- Never use first names unless invited to do so.
- Germans answer the phone by giving their name.
- Space is sacred. Germans seldom invite people to their homes. They have a very strong sense of privacy.
- Germans use direct eye contact but do not like touching. They do not smile readily and gestures are restrained.
- German managers tend to keep office doors closed. They believe this minimizes interruptions. Never open a door without knocking.
- German use formal greetings.
- Discipline and restraint are encouraged.
- Top management dresses much more conservatively than middle management and non-professionals.

# U.S. Gestures

- Americans tend to stand an arms length away from each other.

- Americans generally respect queues or lines. To shove or push one's way into a line will often result in anger and verbal complaint.

- Beckoning is done by raising the index finger and curling it in and out, or by raising the hand and curling the fingers back toward the body.

- Using the hand and index finger to point at objects or to point directions is common.

- Whistling is a common way to get the attention of someone at a distance.

- "No" is signalled by waving the forearm and hand (palm out) in front and across the upper body, back and forth.

- Americans use the standard OK sign, the V for victory sign and the thumbs up sign.

## German Gestures

- A firm handshake with every person you meet is customary.

- Germans do not like to see people place their feet on office furniture.

- Chewing gum (or anything else) is considered impolite for professionals.

- To wave goodbye, extend the hand upward, palm out and wave the fingers up and down.

- Waving the hand back and forth means "no."

- To signal the number "one," hold the thumb upright.

- To signal "good luck," Germans make two fists with thumbs tucked inside other fingers and then make a motion like they are pounding lightly on a surface.

- Sometimes at a large dinner table it is awkward to reach across the table to shake hands so people will just rap their knuckles slightly on the table as a form of greeting to others.

- The OK gesture is considered rude among the more cultured.

- Putting your hands in your pockets while talking is impolite.

# Communication Interferences

Effective communication, both verbal and nonverbal, means that the sending and processing of information between people, countries and businesses is understood, examined, interpreted, and responded to in some way. Any factor that causes a barrier or eliminates the successful transmission of information is defined as a communication interference.

- **Environmental interference** is an actual physical disturbance in the environment such as power outage, unregulated temperatures, a person or group talking very loud, etc.

- **Physiological interference** can be a hearing loss, laryngitis, illness, stuttering, neurological or organic deficit, etc.

- **Semantic interference.** We understand a word to have a certain meaning but the other person has a different meaning. Body language and gestures mean different things to different people. This includes confusion of abbreviated organizational jargon and pronunciation. Universal meanings (semantic understanding) are rare.

- **Syntactic interference.** Words are placed in certain order to give our language meaning. If the words are out of order, the meaning may be changed (this includes grammar).

- **Organizational interference.** Ideas being discussed lack sequence and can't be followed.

- **Psychological interference.** Words that incite emotion are used. In any emotional state (positive or negative) emotions need to be diffused in order to communicate effectively.

- **Social interference.** This includes cultural manners that are inappropriate for the country such as accepted codes for dress, business etiquette, communication rules, or social activity.

Always become well informed about the customs and culture and get information before you try and do business in another country. Review this book and decide which areas of communication you and your colleagues will have difficulty with in Germany. Anticipate and plan accordingly.

As the visitor to another country, you must move out of your "comfort zone." Make the people from that country feel comfortable doing business with you.

No one country has a lock on world markets. Fundamental changes have occurred in the world economy in the last decade. New technologies, and low labor costs often give nations that once were not major players an advantage. This results in increased competition. Yet international business is vital to any country's prosperity.

Business is conducted by people and the future of any country in a global economy will lie with people who can effectively think and act across ethnic, cultural and language barriers. We need to understand that the differences between nations and cultures is profound. The European-based culture of the United States has very different values and behaviors than other cultures in the world. If you cannot accept and adapt to these differences, you will not succeed.

Companies striving to market their business overseas can become truly successful only when they recognize that the key is operating with sensitivity toward the culture and communication of the other country. Communication cannot be separated from culture and this is true when doing business in other countries.

No flourishing company would present themselves to another company their own country without researching that company's business culture and adapting their image to meet the customer's comfort level. It's the same when doing business in another country. You must adapt your image by using your knowledge of effective cultural communication to present a positive public image to the other country.

The first thing is to identify your target audience: clients, customers, suppliers, financial people, government employees and so on. Then you must learn how to effectively communicate with them, and this means learning the culture.

Business failure internationally rarely results from technical or professional incompetence. It is often due to a lack of understanding of what people from other countries want, how they work and so on. This lack of understanding can put a company at a tremendous disadvantage.

Learning the business protocol and practices of the country where you want to do business can give you great leverage. The more you know about the people you do business with, the more successful you can be. Businesspeople must make every contact they have with a foreign customer or business partner a positive one. Business leaders and managers must rethink the way they do business in the new global marketplace.

## Succeeding in International Business

To be successful in the global market, you must:

- **Be flexible.** Cultural adaptations are necessary for both countries to get along and do business. Resisting the local culture will only lead to distrust.

- **Have patience.** Adjust your planning. Initiating business in many countries takes a long range approach and may require two or three years. Anticipate problems and develop alternative strategies.

- **Prepare thoroughly.** Research the country, the organization, the culture and beliefs of the people you will be dealing with.

- **Know your bottom line.** Know exactly what you want from a deal and at what point an agreement is not in your best interest. Know when to walk away.

- **Form relationships.** Encourage getting involved with the new community if you're going to be in the country for a long period.

- **Keep your cool.** Pay attention to the wide range of national, cultural, religious and social differences you encounter.

■ **Show respect.** Search for the other side's needs and interests. Accentuate the positive. Don't preach your own beliefs and respect their beliefs.

When you are using this book, review your own beliefs and values about correct business protocol and ethics. Then match these ideas with the business practices and protocol in Germany.

You can contribute to your own success by recognizing that you will have to move out of your own "comfort zone" of doing business into the cultural business zone of Germany in order to develop the rapport necessary to meet the needs of your client or partner. This does not mean you compromise your company's image or product but that you do business following Germany's protocol while there. It's only for a short time that you may be following their rules, and the payoff can be one in which concepts can be sold while still maintaining a consistent image and approach that is culturally appropriate.

## Quick Tips: United States

- The United States is a very ethnically diverse country. To do business, it is important to be open to this diversity and to be flexible.

- Americans tend to be very individually oriented and concerned with their own careers. Their first loyalty is to themselves.

- Americans want to be liked. They prefer people who are good team players and want to cooperate.

- Americans value equality and dislike people who are too status or rank conscious.

- Most Americans are open, friendly, casual and informal in their manners. They like to call people by their first names quickly.

- Americans like to come right to the point and are uncomfortable with people who are indirect and subtle.

- Americans expect people to speak up and give their opinions freely and to be honest in the information they give. They like a direct and specific "yes" or "no."

- Americans can be very persistent. When they conclude a business transaction and sign a contract, they expect it to be honored. They do not like people who change their minds later.

- Be punctual.

- Put it in writing. Germans like to have things written down. Written contracts are important.

- Cut out the glitz. Germans do not like a lot of boasting or flashy presentations. They like facts and details and an emphasis on quality. They pay a lot of attention to order and planning.

- Respect the hierarchy. Rank is important to the Germans and information and decisions must go through the proper chain of command.

- Slow down. Germans like to take their time in making decisions. Do not attempt to rush them with a hard sell approach.

## Common Phrases

| | |
|---|---|
| *Good morning* | Guten Morgen |
| *Good afternoon* | Guten Tag |
| *Good evening* | Guten Abend |
| *My name is* | Ich heisse |
| *What is your name?* | Wie heissen Sie? |
| *I'm pleased to meet you* | Ich freue mich Sie Kennenzulernen |
| *How are you?* | Wie geht es Ihnen? |
| *Fine, thank you* | Gut, danke |
| *You are welcome* | Bitte (sehr) |
| *Excuse me* | Verzeihung |
| *Please* | Bitte |
| *Thank you* | Danke (sehr) |
| *Yes/No* | Ja/Nein |
| *Goodbye* | Auf Wiedersehen |
| *Mr/Mrs/Miss* | Herr/Frau/Fraulein |

Available in this series:

Business China

Business France

Business Germany

Business Japan

Business Mexico

Business Taiwan

For more information, please contact:

Sales and Marketing Department
NTC Publishing Group
4255 West Touhy Avenue
Lincolnwood, IL 60646
708-679-5500